Dedications

To my precious Baby Jake who has taught me how to see the world in a new light and how truly blessed we are. ~AGS

To my grandmother, Zelda Silberstein. ~JM

4RV Publishing LLC,
2912 Rankin Terrace, Edmond OK 73013
http://4rvpublishing.com

Illustrations copyright © 2015 by Jessica McClure and 4RV Publishing
Book Design: Aidana WillowRaven
Editor-in-Chief: Vickey Malone Kennedy

ISBN-13: 978-1-940310-26-8

4RV Children's Corner
Printed in the United States of America.

My Name is JAKE

hello

By Angela Graham Steele
illustrated by Jessica McClure

Children's Corner

Hi, my name is Jake.
Did you know that God made me extra special?

Most people have a total of 46 chromosomes.

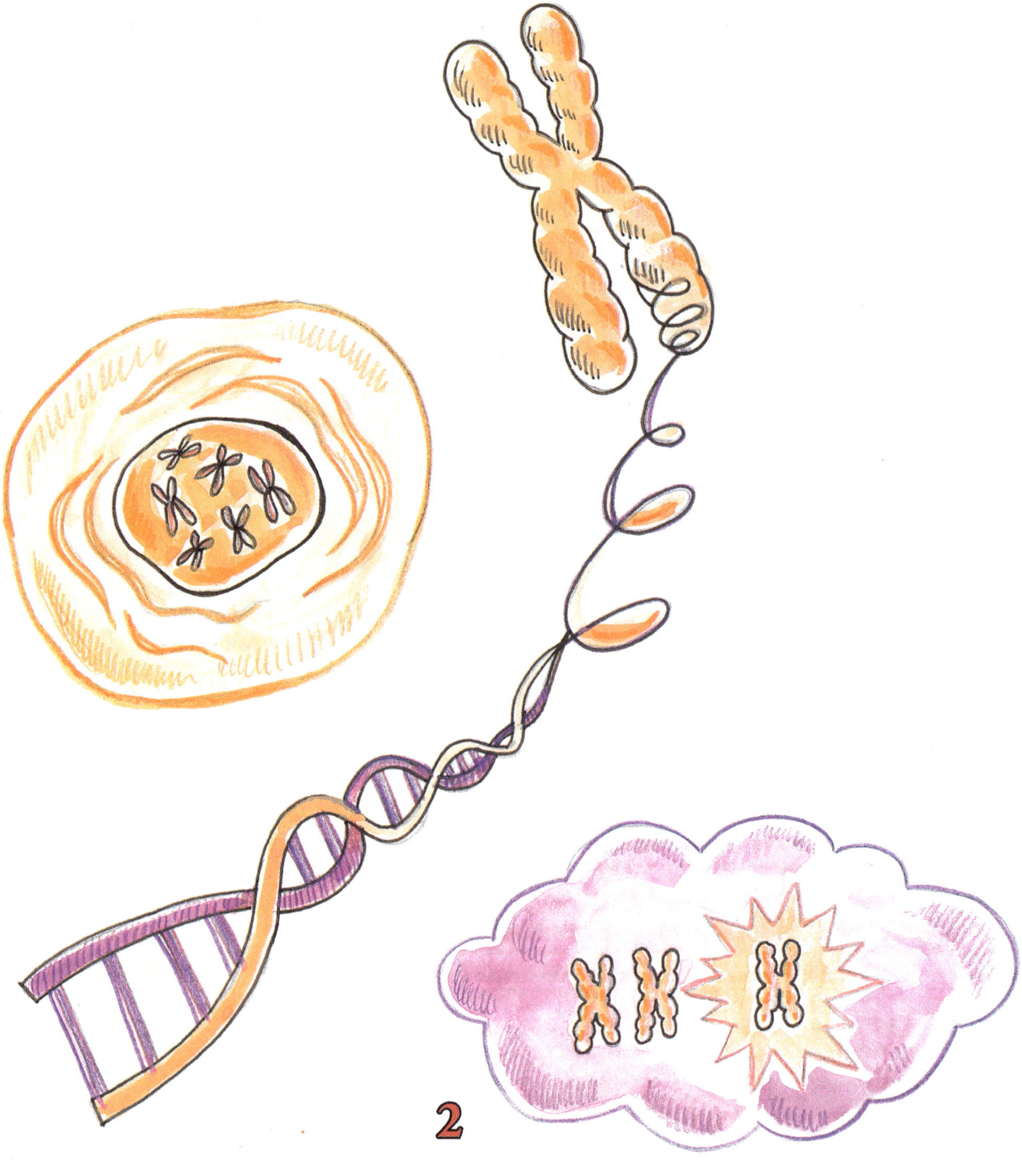

2

I have 47 ... a pretty lucky number if you ask me.

I have an extra 21st Chromosome.
That means I have what is called Down Syndrome.

You might notice some things about me that are different,

but really, we are a lot alike.

5

I like to play ball. Do you?

I like to play with my brothers.

Do you like to play?

I like cats and dogs.

9

Especially, when my dog licks my face.

I like to learn new things and explore.

I like to have friends.

Do you?

13

I like to swing at the playground.

15

I like to watch television.

Do you?

I like to go to church
with my family and read
the Bible.

I like to say the prayer before each meal.

19

I like to get kisses and hugs from Mommy and Daddy.

Do you?

God made us all different.
Some of us have brown eyes, while others have blue eyes.

Some of us have black hair or red hair or yellow hair or brown hair,

and some people even have purple hair.

Still, we are more alike than we are different.

27

Bio Angela Graham Steele

Angela Graham Steele and her husband have four boys and reside in Washington, Oklahoma on a small farm. Her youngest son Jake was born in December of 2009 with Down Syndrome. She hopes to teach others about the joys of loving a child with an extra chromosome and is an advocate for teaching children that "although we may all be different in one way or another, our hearts remain the same."

Angela received her B.A. in Communications from Park University in Parkville, Missouri. She is an active member of the Down Syndrome Association of Central Oklahoma and First Baptist Church of Washington. Angela is an avid reader, and she enjoys taking care of her animals on the farm, volunteering in her community, watching her boys play sports, and spending time with her family. She and her family operate Steele Family Farm and make Handcrafted Goat Milk Soap.

Bio Jessica McClure

Jessica McClure currently lives in Maryland where she works as a plush toy designer at a company called The Petting Zoo. She attended Pratt Institute in Brooklyn, NY to earn her BFA in illustration and enjoys spending time with her family.

Acknowledgements

.

Thank you to our family, friends, church family, and community who have shown us tremendous support and love during our difficult journeys and celebrating with us during our triumphs. Thank you for loving us…and most of all, thank you for loving and embracing Jake.

CPSIA information can be obtained at www.ICGtesting.com
Printed in the USA
LVOW01s0353190515

438929LV00001B/1/P